Reconciliation In Action

by

Sadie Naomi Findlater Williams

authorHOUSE®

AuthorHouse™
1663 Liberty Drive, Suite 200
Bloomington, IN 47403
www.authorhouse.com
Phone: 1-800-839-8640

First published by AuthorHouse 8/8/2007

ISBN: 978-1-4343-1449-9 (sc)
ISBN: 978-1-4343-1448-2 (hc)

Printed in the United States of America
Bloomington, Indiana

This book is printed on acid-free paper.

Acknowledgement

In the process of my writing these pages, I acknowledge that I could not venture out into the world of putting my thoughts and ideas down on paper, without the guidance of, the mighty source of my being (God). The guiding spirit of his omnipresence leads the way as my focus steadily communicates with His presence that is within me. I therefore write about the things, of which I perceive.

A special thank you, to one of my Sunday-school teachers, formerly a retired English teacher, (Ms. Mary Newby); who lovingly scanned through many of the written pages, and polished some areas that needed clarity; thereby, helping to make this book note-worthy.

I believe that the compelling power of the mind can demonstrate control in various and most incredible ways. One may ask how is this possible? The answer is: it belongs to the one individual, and no one else can operate this incredible masterpiece. God has created a built-in mechanism that every person possesses. It can be used to the individual's advantage or disadvantage at the age of accountability. The power of control is the built-in thought process that an individual is at privilege to operate in his or her waking and conscious life. In the moment of applying this control, words or action, good or bad makes its appearance. It is by choosing to control the thought process that will reveal the impact of the thought process positive, or negative. The choice of action made can affect the individual's life, or lives of others. Deliberate angry words and action, can sometimes be excused, by using this precious little word known as **sorry,** when expounded with passion. However, angry words and acts of abuse can leave its scars on the offender, as well as the victim, that may last for a long, long time. As you read, this book, you may discover "Food for thought". You may even want to make notes, and give your own views of the thoughts and ideas presented by the Author, for your reading discernment.

Reconciliation
In
Action

Contents

Remembering many -
Essential welcomed -
Changes in -
Offering of -
Numerous practical -
Choice with -
Inclusion of -
Light service -
Ideal for -
Action and -
Trust regarding -
Important practical -
Order to -
Nurture always -

These are nuggets of Excellence

Introduction

In this book the principal topic is the word **Reconciliation**; which refers to some decision-making processes of ideas such as, doing kind acts, and settling indifferences with a desire to maintain one's own peace of mind. Peace of mind allows an individual to accept closure to a present or past conflict, thereby influencing others to reach an accepted agreement toward peace. It also characterizes personal decision to peacefully lay aside emotional issues in order for the mind to accept closure, and loyalty to maintain that order of conduct to one's own self.

People can be hurt mentally as well as physically from various incidents that may occur in their lives. It takes direct effort of an individual to get rid of unhealthy thoughts. This will happen by reconstructing the old billboard of the past, with renewed and positive involvement that will create constructive change in thoughts and actions. Reconciliation is a decisive condition of the mind that is able to identify, capture and quench, unwanted thoughts, while maintaining good thoughts that are constructive and healthy for every-day living.

Good judgment with self-discipline and order is always necessary to achieve practical goals and objectives. The topic of each of the following paragraphs begins with words that the writer uses to describe each alphabet that spells out the word, **R-E-C-O-N-C-I-L-I-A-T-I-O-N,** to express its nuggets of excellence.

Remembering

Remembering a crisis occurrence that time cannot erase from the mind is usually a memory that will sometimes last for a lifetime. Some people deal with the problem by seeking psychological counseling to bring closure to their condition. Some find comfort in prayer for healing through God, while others seek to control their fears by seeking medical treatment. Whatever method the individual uses to find comfort, there has to be an approach to which the state of mind will reach its reconciliation. If an individual turns to alcohol or drugs to avoid **remembering** the sad past, further damage can happen that results in habit forming that weakens the mind and creates addiction; whereby the thought process will return, when reality finds its way back into **remembering** the problem. I believe that the most sensible thing to do is to allow the mind to get to the point of reconciliation, whereby a peaceful acceptance of the memory is treated, and put to its rest. Many people find different ways to deal with unwanted stresses, these realities of life can happen. I find that a good night's sleep is essential for body, soul and spirit. I believe that comedy sometimes plays an important role in alleviating stress, because it promotes laughter. A good belly laugh is like medicine to the mind; the belly laugh moves the frame of your belly into motion that stimulates the mental. Dancing and exercise create their own rewards. Music, especially melodious music, is good at any hour of the day or night; it creates a peaceful calm. Take a walk, and keep a song in your heart, pray always, and maintain a peaceful attitude. It is a resolute fact, of how the mental receives transformation when the mind accepts peace, in **remembering** that this affirms the resolve and stability that *reconciliation* offers.

Essential

It is **essential** for the mind to cultivate the value known as reconciliation. There is no better feeling that gives peace and control of one's emotion, than getting to a level of a controlled frame of mind. It is **essential** to move the mind to its highest level of determination that offers a cure for unrest. Life with its many changes, and challenges, sometimes propel an individual into the unexpected. Whether or not it is good or bad, it is **essential** to seek the peace that reconciliation offers when the emotional battery drains itself. One does not have to look very far; it is as close as closing the eyes to achieve a quiet moment. Think of the **essential** possibilities that can break through when you greet your new day. It is **essential** to keep a positive attitude. A Good attitude will pave the way to a successful life. The good Lord declares in his holy word according to (Ephesians 4-32,) that we should "*Be kind one to another*". Blessings can break through when we least expect. Every individual mind has its own trait. One can only imagine how confusing life would really be if every individual thought process were the same. We are a unique, yet diverse people. I see us as God's beautiful rose garden on earth, of many flowers in different colors, shapes, and sizes. Together we do make a beautiful bouquet of flowers for the beauty of the world and for our Creator, (God). So sad are the flower devoured by thorns that will not take its place in His bouquet, to give Him pleasure. The glory of God's creation is all around us, as we bask in the wonderful sunlight of his blessings. It is a spiritual concept of the golden rule_to be a brother's keeper at some time and point of life, regardless of language, class or ethnic creed. Humane acts of kindness will leave golden footprints on the road of life to give essential sanctity of peace that offers *reconciliation*.

Changes

Changes that may occur in the everyday activities of an individual can sometimes bring welcome as well as unwelcome conditions. Some will create joy, or obscurity, while dealing with them individually. After measuring in detail all areas, there has to be a closure to create reconciliation. Take for example that a professional individual is faced with making a decision that requires relocating to a new job site of a company's employ, that may also mean finding a new place to live. That may also be a requirement in order for proper development and growth to happen. When one can welcome **change** as a good thing, there can be joyous celebrations to honor the occasion. Benefit and reward for someone making the **change**, can very well be financial achievements, or environmental conditions. If there are undesirable conditions such as having to deal with an indifferent neighbor at the new place, there may be some element of uneasiness that create unpleasant situation. To resolve the issue, one may choose to live in denial, or apply resolve to create peace of mind. In a situation such as this, there is not always an easy way out. My idea of how to handle this **change** of the unpleasant issue, and how to create a peaceful environment with the indifferent neighbor, is to apply obedience to the golden rule. It is often quite rewarding to note, how a soft answer can **change** an angry foe into believing that things are not always as bad as they may be seen to be, even if it appears to be an illusion of high hopes. There is always a possibility whereby the mental concept can accept a compromise between neighbors, to resolve differences in accepting wholesome **change** of heart that achieve a spiritual calm to receive and embrace the peace of *reconciliation.*

Offering

Offering in service of goodwill by those who go the extra mile to help in a humane act of kindness is truly priceless. Many go the extra mile by putting their own lives in danger to contribute **offering** of kindness. Such an **offering** is sometimes spontaneous acts of bravery in order to save lives. Offerings rendered in variety of ways, in words, finances, or deeds, can prove to be of priceless importance. Words of worth, spoken in the true context of goodwill, may be received by those who diligently listen and receive the message that changes their lives. As words of kindness are passed on among people, gestures of goodwill can also create transformation and change of attitudes and behavior, to those who receive messages of spoken words, and who apply them to their lives, to create meaningful exchange within their community. Words can create healing as well as curses. Sincere **offerings** of kind words are like seeds that will grow and flourish on fertile soil when sown in love. Words of hate spoken can create chaos and distortion of a people. Words can kill, and words can cure. Many financial offerings are contributions made to support the survival of hurting people, and many go the extra mile in their giving which proves to be priceless because the recipients face overwhelming needs, which only that extra mile of financial **offering** could really create the necessary change. Many people give of their time in **offering** service to help those who may be in distress-who truly need some personal support from someone, in order for them to find their way out of a critical time of distress, and who truly need a shoulder to lean on.

The words of Jesus as recoded in the Holy Bible, (Acts 20:35,) *"It is more blessed to give than to receive."* This very important act of contributing to needs, achieves meaningful results for both the giver and the receiver. These unselfish contributions justify the true spirit of kindness, whereby together we can participate in the joys of **offering** to the cause of humanity, and receive the peace of *reconciliation.*

Numerous

Numerous talents are recognized as natural gifts, endowed to humans by God the Creator that can be developed in their specialized area of talents and skills, with help and study through science and technology. While having the potential to invent and produce, **numerous** important products can become available for use to the public. Some medical break-through, are used to promote healthy living that maintains longevity. In exploring the outer space environments and receiving valuable information, scientists are able to continue further study to develop their **numerous** areas of talent and skills. It is less difficult for some people who have the gift of **numerous** natural talents to express their craft with undeniable efficiency, enthusiasm and success. Some individuals who are talented, and who possess the power of speaking for hours, can capture the attention of an audience while mastering their craft with little or no discomfort. Some singers will master their craft of singing, to delight their listener with numerous renditions. Comedy and sports are some sought after entertainment that interest people of all ages. The talent of compiling common words used to create poetic message, is an art that is express and written by those who deliver their poetic messages to exhibits delightful stirs.

The **numerous** gifts and talents of aspiring individuals served humanity throughout the ages. Unfortunately, some never have the opportunity to develop their natural talent; but everyone has, in some way, something to offer.

Birds and beasts, and all living creatures perform in their own **numerous** and natural ways. Even trees and flowers have something to offer in their own ways. These **numerous** natural gifts are blessings, seen in our world of complexities, as we continue to share them, on the journey of life, to experience and accept the true sense of *reconciliation.*

Choice

A **choice** is an act to determine a preference that represents a decision based on willingness to accept the decision of preference. The result can turn out to be favorable, but can also present undesirable conditions. It is very important to think carefully, and evaluate a situation, before making important decisions. There should also be willingness to accept the outcome, good or bad. One must therefore be careful to use good judgment, while in the process of making a **choice**. The thought process conveys messages from the eye, and the ear, to the mind. The mind determines how to deliver the course of action that will perform its intention. For instance, I need to make a decision to shop for apparel. In the process of deciding where to locate the most suitable store for this transaction, I must make a **choice** based on the most practical location where I may find what I need. I make the decision and I am satisfied with my **choice**. Off then I go. I get to my destination and prepare to bargain hunt. After examining carefully the various designs and sizes, I make my **choice** on the garment that is just right for my budget, and I am satisfied: "mission accomplished". Some choices may prove to be significantly rewarding. Some may create failure and regret-whereby the disappointment lingers in the mind for a long time. It can be very easy to overlook defects in something that involves making a right **choice**, especially those that involve love, romance and marriage. Good **choice** creates joy and fulfillment. Therefore, it is of great importance to use good judgment in making a decisive **choice**; and by so doing it will lead to the satisfying joy and peace, of *reconciliation*.

Inclusion

Inclusion is a decisive acknowledgement that attaches someone or something to an already existing establishment. **Inclusion** may be an act of giving a surprise opportunity for an individual to participate, and to receive acceptance, as a valued participant within a group's activities. **Inclusion** can also be added information based on a story of importance that can have an impact on a particular community of people. When an act of **inclusion** involves people, whether or not it is a public or private matter, a clear indication of the matter becomes part of the determined process. **Inclusion** can happen in agreement of added information to a preexisting package. **Inclusion** can create self-confidence, to individuals who receives the opportunity of participating in important activities. They may even become involved in making much valuable contribution to the cause in which they serve. A society may sometimes overlook the needs of the less fortunate because of little or no representation, and there may be difficulty getting proper recognition, when the law of equal opportunity is not recognized and enforced. In a family matter that involves issues in which a family member were denied information that should have been made available, but were not given the fair share, things can get unpleasant for everyone involved in the matter. In that case, inclusion might have helped to justify adequate relationship, for agreeable unity, and understanding. Institutions, large or small, knows the importance of having board meetings, which may happen on a specified times at an appropriate location.

Interaction keeps the members informed while in the process of getting together, in sharing new information that could be valuable to improve the progress and growth of their company. **Inclusion** is a perfect example of how an acceptance of goodwill helps to cure anxiety and fears and allow growth and transformations. It gives purpose and meaningful acceptance that aspires to consider and affirm **inclusion** as an import concept, to claim the joy of *reconciliation*.

Light

Light is one of God's most priceless creations endowed to humankind. He created **light** on the first day of his Majestic and Infinite Work. According to The King James Version of the Holy Bible, this proclamation of God's words declares the creation of light (Genesis 1:3), God spoke these commanding words; He said, "*LET THERE BE LIGHT*": and there was light. These awesome words brought light into being. God saw that it was very good! The illumination of **light** will penetrate the most darkened areas of any place on earth. God created the light in its glorious splendor! The morning sun so brilliant the naked eyes cannot dare to gaze upon it as it rises on the eastern horizon and brightens the earth. The marvelous moon that lights up the night sky, and stars that twinkle like diamonds in the darkness of the sky. The distinctive principle of **light** is to bring clarity to things hidden in the dark. Thomas Edison with his amazing insight and perseverance to invent and develop electric light would never know that in doing so, civilization would evolve into the different types of technology that exist only by the use of electricity that serves today's generations of the world. Many individuals share the blessing of the abundance of knowledge to establish technology by means of electricity that has become a necessity in almost all areas of life. The use of electric energy has become a great source, used for the operation of modern equipment. Electric lighting is a popular source, often used to decorate in celebration of seasonal events. We must, therefore give respect, and thankfulness, for this great irreplaceable source that is called **Light.**

A spiritual aspect of light as mentioned in the Holy Bible as revealed in the King James version of (Matthew Chapter 5:16,) which reads as follows, "*Let your light so shine before men, that they may see your good works and glorify your father which is in Heaven*". This statement spoken by the Lord Jesus Christ in his teachings to demonstrate spiritual Light is recognized, and revered by Christians who feel blessed and enhanced in accepting this spiritual **Light**, and satisfaction that offers the peace of *reconciliation.*

Ideal

Ideal is an idea or action in display that represents a decision-making process. For instance, I needed to find and establish a facility in an environment suitable for me to accommodate and care for displaced children, who are wards of the state. I must put into action the idea, in order to find the ideal facility that I desire to have. After a diligent search, I found the **ideal** setting, which is a place far away from the crowded city. My idea put into action, produced a satisfactory result. The facility and location offered the **ideal** space and environment that is conducive to the growth and the development for growing children. I went out shopping for a Christmas tree. It had to be a certain size that would fit into the space in my house where I wanted it to be. My idea was then set into action. After a tiresome search, I found the ideal Christmas tree of my choice. My idea to search for the Christmas tree allowed me to pursue and accomplish that mission. I decided to have lunch outdoors with my children. It was a very hot day; fortunately, I found an **ideal** spot under the spread branch of a very large oak tree in the backyard. We sat and ate there together while a cool gentle breeze lends us its tender touch. We had fun together exchanging funny jokes. This idea set in action created a united engagement at lunchtime. Following the successful events, I realize that I made some **ideal** choices based on my needs. Even though it was hard work doing all the things that I set out to do I knew that it was all worth my effort, because I was able to give joy to many others who needed me at that time. My accomplishment gave me the ideal satisfaction that I needed, and allowed me to enjoy the peace of *reconciliation*.

Action

Action is a display of spoken words, documentations, as well as performance of something in the physical. Individual/s may use their knowledge to perform in visible showings. Performance that require writing, or verbal exchange, are displayed in various areas to become physical performance, as expressed in action that may vary in ways that are useful for every-day transactions. Words can express ideas by writing that which the mental transmits. The educational system of cultures of the world allows educators to translate their work in many different languages, as recorded in books, to use for study guide. These educators devote their time and intellectual ability to deliver information that who-so-ever chose to broaden their horizon in acquiring such knowledge; can take advantage of the opportunity to learn various languages. The eyes see, the ears hear, while the hands relay in writing, information from the eyes and the ears. The action of these members of the body helps all the other members to serve the purpose that expresses movements that is call action; for which God intends it, in an orderly display. When one organ of the body is unable to function normally, the entire operating system can feel its effect. Scientists take **action** in continually exploring and studying the operation, and performance, on how the different organs of the body function. God has created this marvelous body masterpiece with all its intricate parts that function and operate in its incredible uniqueness and unison. Medical Technology and Science help doctors to study the function of the body, in order to determine causes of various diseases that can affect the human body. In using medical equipment to examine and see the internal areas, they can detect an affected organ's malfunction. There are times when it is important and necessary to take **action** in correcting breeches to which a problem of physical failure of an organ of the body requires medical treatment, to help repair a defective organ.

Action can deliver positive results when guided in the right direction. The complexity of the human body is something that God has created to perform in its five senses (to see, to hear, to feel, to taste, to smell.) these senses are designed to operate in unison: whereby individuals can detect when something is wrong with the way the body feels. Important studies in the area of medical technology can achieve favorable or unfavorable prognosis that will show up in an individual's medical record. When a medical test of an individual happens, physicians evaluate result of tests to give information on how to treat the patient. Some of these treatments often allow individual/s to enjoy a healthier, longer life. There are many areas of study in the medical profession, and each area has its own function. The world has people who are capable to operate in their individual capacity and areas of skill that create valuable result in every conceivable ways of life. We are all in the daily process of taking **action** in our own individual way, and capability. We should therefore give thanks, and appreciate our own uniqueness in our **action,** while accepting the joy of *reconciliation.*

Trust

Trust is a feeling that can help to create a peaceful state of mind. It can shape individual/s lives to their highest level of confidence, to produce visions of hope and sanctity to those who enjoy their special joy of trust. **Trust** in action can relate its worth of belonging, by the characteristic behavior of individual/s. **Trust** between individuals is essential for bonding that creates closeness. It goes hand in hand like partnership between two people in agreement of marriage. It is an undeniable social standard, which can reveal its worth between individual/s in relationship. Giving respect in pleasant attitude in dealing with others, can pave the way for positive response of acceptance. When **trust** between individuals is done in verbal agreement, it is a bond to be honored with sincerity, and should be a sacred law that begins with ones own self. The Shakespearian screen play, (Hamlet,) an allegory of Shakespeare's memorable statement, depict these following words, **"To thine own self be true and it shall follow as the night, the day; thou canst not then be false to any man"**. **Trust** is an important ingredient that creates fulfillment between people in a unified manner. In the Holy Bible, there are many references regarding **trust.** One example can be found in the King James version of (Psalm 17:7,) which reads as follows, **"Shew thy marvelous loving-kindness, O thou that savest by thy right hand them which put their** trust **in thee from those that rise up against them."** When **trust** funds are establish in support of particular individuals, or organizations, they are set up in order to maintain a certain level of organized contribution of property or finance, governed by the principles of the rule of law. The power of **trust** reflects some underlining principles that embrace giving, and the ability to accept a satisfying conclusion of what it takes to acquire the joy of trust and fulfillment, of *reconciliation*.

Important

Important is a word sometimes used to express urgency; and it can deliver messages of valuable information. For instance, people who work in executive positions, such as the news media, and who may have to deal with the public every day, usually have the opportunity of delivering information of urgency to the public that may affect a nation. **Important** information broadcast by means of Radio, Television, and Computer-Internet, sends its messages within minutes to alert people of up-to-date events and stories that can save lives. This undoubtedly can affect an entire nation. It is **important** for people to know about things that are happening around the world, and in their neighborhood. The news media is a necessary source of getting news to the public. Mail carriers' jobs require a great deal of diligence and care to make sure that mails are delivered correctly and in a timely manner, to individuals at their proper addresses. It is very **important** to maintain a clean environment: and workers, who are designated to keep the streets of inner city neighborhoods clean, serve in a very **important** operation that has to be maintained on a daily basis. A clean environment gives reflection on the community of people, and it is good to note that people need to be responsible for keeping their own **important** space clean; in order to maintain a healthy and desirable appearance.

All professions and skills are required to fit into various administrative divisions of society that gives services for the good of its citizens. The world need Teachers, Lawyers, Doctors, Writers, Ministers, Architects, Carpenters Financial advisors, Public Service workers, and anyone who is capable of offering services for the good of people. We live in a world of give and take. Each individual plays an **important** role of service as we travel together on the journey that involves life. These are manifested blessings of God that can help us to recognize the importance of working together, with a true spirit to recognize, and experience the Important joy of *reconciliation.*

Order

Order is a required process to keep performance in togetherness that will always be necessary to prevent chaotic occurrence. The governing body of a society must have and maintain its law based on an **order** of united principles to differentiate between right and wrong. Information written and enforced by a governing body of some elected individuals, relay the law in written document. People of the society are therefore required to recognize and understand the law as written. It then becomes necessary for people of the society to obey the law that is designed to promote **order** in its respective manner. In all areas of living, things must have a formidable foundation for proper operation whether it is with work or play. There is a principal **order** by which to be born, that takes each individual from stage to stage throughout life's existence. Each individual must first be born for the life's growth process to begin. As soon as birth happens the growing process will continue, while the aging stages gradually creeps in. This is the intent by which God has designed the characteristic of life, to maintain **order** in the event of birth, growth and development. One can be fortunate to have longevity by giving attention to apply valuable health care and maintenance to the body. Modern science in medicine has provided valuable information and technical care-giving practices in medicine that may improve the quality and length of life, when administered in its prescribed **order.** God's principle of **order** dominates the planet from sunrise to sunset, in all aspects of his creation, and delivers results, as manifested in every living thing in the world. **Order** can be the state of mind of an individual, who reach a conclusive decision of resolve that was an uncomfortable issue, and decides to embrace a peaceful **orde**r of *reconciliation.*

Nurture

Nurture is a necessary connection that is essential to ensure growth and development. The fulfillment of **nurture** is consistent in human as well as animals. When birth happens, whether it is of man or beasts, it is the beginning of life. Life at this early stage of existence is very fragile for all species, whether or not it is human, or animals. To nurture life, means special attentiveness and care at the beginning in order to maintain healthy growth. For those who initiate nurturing whether or not it is dealing with human lives or protecting a favorite pet animal, the rewards can be very meaningful. Hardships and failure to cope with unexpected challenges can come at any time in life. It is in the difficult times within family, or friends, and even within a community of people that special attention given, can bring healing and restoration. Together, people can work in giving attention and support when necessary to do so. It is essential when facing the hardship of going through, or recovering from a diversity of distresses, that people need each other to work together in order to improve conditions, and extend moral support. Attention is required to **nurture**, strengthen, and preserve the existence of life. The result of saving lives, and the process of nurturing, can create harmony among people that produces long lasting memories. Nurturing is a presentation of hands and hearts working together to bring about productive results. Animals will watch over their young and will even become aggressive in protecting them. The display of nurturing is seen everyday in the activities of human and animals. To **nurture** is to give comfort and assurance, while receiving the reward and fulfillment in the result that comes with *reconciliation*. "These are nuggets of excellence"

The Journey

As we journeyed through the previous chapters, we saw that the fourteen (14) alphabets taken from the word reconciliation, displayed the fourteen chosen words used, to suggest some of the meaningfulness of the word. (**Reconciliation.**) The words, as relayed in sequential order, convey ideas that relates to reconciliation. Those words expressed ideas as seen through the eyes of the Author, throughout each of the chapters. Reference and comments made of the word give some of its meaningful attributes, of acknowledgment.

I chose to write about reconciliation after experiencing two flooding disasters to my home between the years of 2002-2005, while having to confront some family issues that I was facing at that time. In those floorings, I lost many irreplaceable and valuable items I collected over the years; but worst of all, was the loss of the entire office documents and equipment of my organization that took twelve years to get to where it was, all covered under the flowing deposits. The 2005 flood swept trough just after I got my house repaired from the previous flooding, although with less intensity. Once again, I grieved at my loss of having to remove newly installed carpet among other items. I had my moments when nothing seemed real to me anymore; but through it all, I became reconciled to the fact that I must seek to have peace of mind in order to preserve my sanity. I reconciled in my mind to maintain the peace that I need to function properly, in order to settle the difficult issues that lingered around me. I declared my resolve, and settled with my emotions to keep the peace that would see me through future phases. I decided that while there is continued life, there is an opportunity to set goals and pursue opportunity.

When an individual is healthy enough to do work, that gives the opportunity to do so: figuratively speaking, that helps to motivate the mind as well as keeping the body active, while deriving social interaction with people.

Sometimes, the aging process takes precedence over what the mind wants the body to pursue, but the strength of the body gets stubborn and gives its limitation, that is quite understandable, and must be given due respect in obeying that command. If the body says keep still and rest, one should be under no obligation to defy that law of nature that is associated with longevity. I believe old age is a blessing, for someone to fall into that category of life.

The wise man Solomon of the Bible, reminds us in (Eccl 3:1), King James Version, that--"*To every thing there is a season, and a time to every purpose under the sun*". Those who have worked throughout their productive years, and have reached the age of retirement, should have the advantage of resting when it is necessary to do so.

I look at life as a journey that goes on from day, to day, as a continuation process. Whether one is old or young, it is every moment that counts.

A healthful quality of life is to be treasured. It is important to be in control of the thought process while using the mind to fulfill the important thought that each moment produces. It is also important to acknowledge the inevitable fact that "tomorrow is promised to no one" therefore, each moment is important. Time allows individuals to set goals and work toward results that can happen in producing positive outcome. Hard work deserves it just reward; but sometimes hard work falls through the cracks of life; leaving the labor, and the laborer to go unfilled of its worth. These are some of the realities of every-day occurrences. Sometimes it requires patience and continued training, in order achieve the necessary results from labor. So let us be thankful for every moment that comes along and do our best to use our time wisely.

Things and time changes as we live our every-day lives; but it do not give excuses for personal corrupt conduct. The law of order will continue to be a concept by which to give justice, in the process of judging between right and wrong. Some laws are subject to change. It may sometimes be necessary to actively review an original law that were chosen, in comparison to what the changing times is offering. In order to keep up with present changes, it may be necessary to adjust the old, to connect with the new changing time. As we live and learn, we know that some of the old ideas worked well for us in the past: but while we give recognition to the old, we learn to connect with the new, and move on in a united attitude.

No one can stop the wind from blowing, and no one can prevent the rain. The use of Science and technology predicts when to expect certain change in weather, even earthquakes, yet no one can prevent the disasters from coming, or even determine how much damage it will leave behind. We however, do our best to find a safe escape and pray that the worst will not happen. Life can present the bitter as well as the sweet. Unexpected incidents can happen, as we live in a fast pace environment. No one will know the result of any disaster until the assessment is made We must do our best to deal with whatever it is that happen, while we seek refuge in peace of mind.

When one can look failure straight in the eye and defy disappointment that come, the struggle to overcome will take strength of character to play its divine role, while allowing the mind to think positive, in overcoming great difficulties.

Unexpected phenomenon can show up in the most dramatic way, to disrupt a day's plan that is set to fulfill certain intended activity. Interruptions can change or slow things down with no previous warning. One of my reflections is my encounter with a rainstorm that brought great big balls of ice, falling from the sky that seemed to have come with its vengeance. I call it the hailing wailing rain. I describe my experience in the following passage that I call, "The hailing wailing rain."

The Hailing Wailing Rain

Rumbling grumbling comes the hailing rain!

Whack! Whack! Whacking, on rooftops it pours

Upon vast fields and everything in its path;

Dousing its icy contents while it condescend

In Brisk downpour it comes, bouncing all around

Landing on whoever, and whatsoever, in its path

Intimidating human's feelings as it creates havoc.

It Scare and bewilders outdoor field animals,

As they prance about not knowing where to go.

While getting relentless beating from the hailing rain

They try to shake off their un-welcomed intruder!

Even humans scramble to get out of its icy path.

So much icy round balls descending in full blast,

Leave indentation on metal and shattered glass;

Creating its icy blanket on landscape all around

In the display of its short-lived mysterious act

Shortly after making its concurred appearance

It puts on its disengaging act, welcoming its exit!

Then all of a sudden it makes its disappearance!

Leaving a welcomed calm in the environment,

Where humans are left bewildered yet relieved

To contemplate nature's act that leaves its memory.

I Watch In Awe

I sometimes watch in awe and astonishment with great sadness in my heart in seeing many television news displaying disaster and loss of lives; I grieved with those who may have experienced the loss of loved ones. I also pray that they may find peace the same way I find reconciliation in many of my distresses. I too know about anxiety and fear, when facing internal emotions, and when it seems as though things just cannot get worse. One can pray individually, also find comfort from others who can help to give prayers and support. Internal disturbances create stress, and stress sometimes reveals change in attitude and behavior. It is good to bear in mind that behind a dark cloud there is a clear blue sky. A good attitude encourages helpful Samaritans who may come along and help to show love; and positive outlook that gives peace of mind, to help overcome the fearful future. The blue sky of life will reveal itself, worrisome moods can change, and sunshine do appear that can brighten the day, as time goes by.

Personally speaking, even though I experienced loss and disappointments I am alive; and in my heart there is a positive feeling: I still hold my dream dear, even though it is temporarily put on hold. The big dream of my life happen to be, to help provide a home for displaced children, who may be separated from their biological homes, because of natural disasters and loss of families. I may not be presently capable, of giving children shelter and care, but I do small services in areas of my capability while I am able to. I also hope that someone who may read what I have written, and who may also encounter disappointments in their lives, will be encouraged to give their service in areas that is possible to give service, and patiently pursue their heart-felt dream. Because while life remain, there can be revealed to them opportunities for their lives, as they continue their journey through life.

The August 29, 2005 disaster, of Hurricane Katrina, happened on a Monday night. Katrina caused death, destruction and devastation that affected many communities in the Gulf Coast region of the U.S.A., and as if that were not enough, Hurricane Rita followed behind Katrina, on Saturday September 24, 2005, creating further destruction. Those two together were the worst disastrous hurricane in the recorded history of America that occurred in that region. This disaster caused tremendous displacement of lives and property. Many thousands of people of the region had to relocate to other communities, and deaths of many hundreds were the beginning of an unforgettable crisis, which will be in the hearts of many, for a lifetime. Many relocate to various unfamiliar communities that change their entire lifestyle. When the Levee broke the floodwater burst through covering houses, cutting off all form of communications. People climbed on rooftops and trees. I watched the news aired on live television, reporting the scene of people waiting for airlift and rescue operation, while others trapped in the dome for days without food and water as they waited for boats to come and rescue them out from the flooded region. Some tried to swim putting their babies in plastic containers that served as makeshift boats as they swam their way to safety. Hundreds perished in the horrific disaster. Such were some of the human suffering, and the struggle to survive. Too numerous to mention are the struggles of those left behind who have lost all of their worldly possession, to face a future of uncertainties. Never-the-less life holds its promise as they dare to overcome, and believe that life is worth the struggle. This unforgettable disaster will bear record in the history books of Historians of the U.S.A., to tell of courageous people who made it out alive from the devastation. Those who perished will be in the memory of many who were families and friends. However difficult survival may appear to be, for them who are still here will need to continue with their lives, as they endeavor to consider finding closure, and seek their peace in *reconciliation.*

Across the world, earthquakes cause thousands of death and destruction, loss of properties, disruption of normal every-day living, and conditions too distressing to describe. Yes, this is our world that encounters natural disasters, and we know that we need to remain strong while we are still alive. There is hope to get over the internal emotional disturbing conditions. Life at its best is very fragile, no one can say for sure how long it will remain within its home (the body). Both of my parents died very young; neither of them lived to see their 40th birthday, however, here I am experiencing my 70th plus which proves that aging is not an heredity condition for me. I am very much here enjoying the blessings called life for which I am very thankful.

As each new day dawns into my life,
I greet the day with thankful prayers
I give reverence to God my Creator
For friends and loved ones I hold dear
If the sun seem to hide its brightness
Because dark clouds dim my view
I know the sun will soon come smiling
When its silvery face shines through
If some annoying snares gets in my way
I will gracefully rise above them all
Because I give reverence to my Creator
When I greet my new day with a prayer

Accountability

I believe that as long as an individual possesses a conscious mind, there is a built-in process of action; which displays itself in the physical that requires accountability. There is always a battle going on within the mind, to differentiate between its display of right and wrong. Under normal circumstance, an unexpected thought may pop-up and manifests itself in words that may offend someone who may be a friend.

Harsh words may inflict painful wounds to someone's heart that cost the dissolution of friendship. Words can also create that never-to-be-forgotten delightful moment that can enrich friendship to last a lifetime. Sometimes it is best to restrain a thought before making open statement that one may later regret. It is not possible to stop thoughts from coming, but one should try to control and examine each thought that pops up, before revealing the thought by action or words. One may need to develop wisdom that will sometimes help with thought-control. The power of thought-control is an absolute gift to those who possess that valuable quality. There is a little voice inside that we call common sense: that can serve as guide that one can use to soften the blow of hasty words that suddenly makes its outburst.

I celebrate life as God's precious gift to humankind; and I give my respect and appreciation, for His wonderful creation. The air I breathe gives maintenance to my life, which is the great mainstream of my survival. I do the best I can to work in areas of my capability. My obedience to the golden rule is to be a brother's keeper when I am able to give my support. It is a good and noble act to lend a helping hand where needed, but it sometimes becomes necessary to say **no** when the helping hand becomes the subject of abuse when misinterpreted. I believe there is a limit to how much the heart can take in any given situation of making personal sacrifices, to help someone. Every individual becomes the product of a society where they reside, by birth, by legal or illegal entry. In a civilize society, every birth is required to be registered at a government's office of registry. Each individual that are Registered gets a legal certificate that gives detail information of their biological offspring, such as their name, date, month, year of birth, and the country of birth, which by right of birth is a citizen of that country. The strength of a nation reflects the wisdom of it leaders. There is not always going to be agreement for individuals to give acceptance and support to an elected individual leader of a particular political party. However, it is very important to be a good law-abiding citizen who will abide by the rule and law of that institution, and give respect to its leaders, as a token of goodwill.

Anger

I believe that some types of anger can justify itself with legitimate reasoning. Those types of anger are sometimes cause by provocation, and deliberate acts, by individual/s who do harm to others, physically, or verbally, to purposely activate strife. In response to a provocation, it may be necessary to cautiously approach the matter of self-defense by quietly disengaging from the immediate confrontation. That is one way of using self-control, to prevent bodily harm. Using a method of timely approach, can justify the outcome to a peaceful settlement. Self-controlled method with good judgment can prevent violent outburst. In some cases, one may just have to use physical separation from the encounter to prevent tragedy from happening. Anger is never good for one's health. Sometimes it takes diligence and lots of patience to deal with grievous situations that create the problem of anger. Too often anger gets out of control, to exhibit its rage in inconceivably violent tragedy, which results in regrets and penance. The cure for anger; is self-control; which is that small voice inside that is too often ignored. Self- control is an internal spirit influence that will work to control anger if the individual will listen and accept its warning signal. Many pain and suffering is sometimes cause by uncontrolled anger The demon known as anger can destroy a nation's meaningful principles, by a Leader's lack of control. Self-defense can express itself in a calm and peaceful manner that brings closure to a dispelled anger. We may not be able to stop a bird from flying over our heads, but we can certainly stop the bird from building its nest on top of our heads. Calm is better than storm, and every heart knows its own soul searching direction, between storm and calm.

No one can predict for sure, something that will happen in the future of one's life, except God; and that is His personal prerogative that He is entitled to, because (He is Creator of the past, present and future.) Each individual is born with a built-in free-will spirit; which allows them to make decisions and choices that may affect their present and future lives. Therefore, good judgment is required when using the freewill concept. There is no point in blaming God when an individual makes bad decisions based on free-will choice that is contrary to both God's laws, and man's laws. In society as I know it to be, if a law is being violated by an individual, there will be a consequence to be reckoned with. In our world today, the purpose of learning to read and write and be trained in different areas of skills, is to know and understand information that are written in books, and being transmitted through the educational system of all countries throughout the world. It is necessary to understand knowledgeable information that may serve as guidelines on how to advance in pursuing undertakings. "I believe that it is a good thing to seek knowledge, because it may prove to be a close companion throughout life. To embrace understanding, as it will prove to be like a best friend that will stand guard in times of needs. To be thankful for each new day and use time wisely: but most of all, how to control these assets with the power that lies within". Time is a precious commodity; wasted time will be gone forever. Every moment's presence is the delivery of time. "Time cannot be harness, or tamed it moves on, and on: and everyone can learn something new in the process of time". "I believe that I should never forget to say, Thank You GOD; for each new day that comes my way; because, it is, His precious gift to me".

Sincerity

I truly believe that sincerity is the best policy in dealing with every-day encounters. A typical example is an individual who makes promises to a voting panel to do the impossible, just because of an ambition, to get elected to an office by deceiving the voters, with false information. After the election when voters find out that they received false information, they loose confidence because of unfulfilled promises. That type of deception is wrong to begin with. Deceptions may also be found in many areas of people to people interactions. Sincerity in essence, is a concept that shows itself in results. This is an outward gesture of fulfillment and truthfulness of promise, or a direct evidence of loyalty to those who may come to expect honesty in a given situation such as, showing acts of kindness and loyalty through friendship between individuals. It is most difficult if not impossible to identify someone's true feelings by mere words. Words needs to be backed-up by a display of willingness to show sincerity in action, which sometimes speaks louder than words. Devotion and forgiveness is healing to the heart; that I believe is a form of expressing sincerity. I believe that the ability to be sincere begins with a willingness to be honest and true to ones own self, as well as with others. If I am angry with myself because of some foolish words spoken that affect another person, I need to show my regret in both words and action. I must also refrain from blaming myself, and redeem my self-image in both the outward showing, and by words. My willingness to prove my sincerity concerning the matter will then earn its merit of trust. My personal thoughts concerning sincerity, is express in the following written poem, as I perceive sincerity.

Sincerity

Sincerity is an expressed form of virtue
It comes with an attitude of thoughtfulness
It is a good feeling that comes from within.
Showing its various outward expressions
When used to fulfill its loyal benediction.
No one knows better than one who imparts it.
And those who are fortunate to receive it
It brings out its beauty that shine like the sun
Brightening the path of the giver, and receiver
Sincerity is truly the voice of honesty in action
It is a good thing to cherish always

Purpose

The purpose of writings is to express acknowledgement of thoughts in action. How a written message is perceive when it appears on paper reflects the idea and thought of the writer. The message bears reflections of the thought's encounters. As the written message appears on paper, views and perception of things, are thereby set in motion. Life is like a mixed diet; we live from day to day in stages of thoughts and ideas. The same way we eat different types of food to sustain life, for development and growth. Our thoughts and ideas will continue as long as it remains conscious, while the process flows on and on, in its living body.

The mind and body are tools that should be use wisely. Individuals have the ability to use the body, and mind, in areas where it can give services. The blessings of being able to see, to hear, to smell, to taste, and to feel, is God's purpose of bringing the body into coordination with each of its functional members, giving fulfillment to His plan for humans on earth. In the process of my writing these pages, I am pursuing my ability to use my functional mind to perform the act of writing with my hands, my eyes and my fingers. The pursuit of knowledge is in the mind of an individual while living and growing mentally and physically. Each individual has his or her own thought-process. It is the thought process that the mind projects that which will make or break the individual.

The thought processes, creates the mechanism by which knowledge is received, as well as transmit its message. Knowledge reveals ingenuity in all aspects of existence of human life on earth. Therefore, as long as life shall last on this planet, ideas will create ingenuity that will burst open the door to new adventure and advancement, in knowledge, and technology. While searching for new channels of adventure throughout my life, I have made different plans that affect my every-day life. While it may sometimes turn out to be learning and growing experiences, my reason for planning, is an effort to get to the next level of my expectation. When I was a young adult, I could deal with long hours of reading and learning different information without tiring; but as I advance in the aging process, I find it much more uncomfortable to prolong my concentration. My body and my eyes have a way of telling me when I have had enough. The dreaded stage of aging carries with it uncertainties of how well the body will continue to maintain mobility. These are very real concerns of those who like me, are advancing through their golden years of **slow downs.**

Although I am not capable of predicting the outcome of my future expectations, the challenge lies with me, whereby I can use my ingenuity in the best way that I know how, to pursue my goals while working toward getting to the next level. When I was a child, I used to sleep and have dreams that seemed so real, that I would wake up and look around to see if the dream that I dreamt was for real. I remember one time when I dreamt that the ground around me was white. In the dream, it appeared as though white clouds were falling to the ground. I woke up to find that everything remained the same. At that time, I lived in a tropical country where the climate remains the same all year round; to me that was very strange. At that time, I had no idea of snow until I grew into adulthood and happened to travel to Canada. That was my very first encounter of real snow, to see, touch and experience it on the ground. Most of all to me is how very cold the weather was there. Many times when I had dreams and other people were involved in my dream I would wait to see if what I encountered with them in the dream would happen the next day: which never did. As I grow older I realize that what I dreamed was not necessarily so in the natural. Many dreams that come to us in the night are indications to remind us that the mind is always active, awake or sleeping.

As the body grows into the aging process, some of its natural resource may be inclined to weaken, loosing its vigorous functioning. This is to remind us that, there is always going to be an end to every good thing, even as time changes by taking us through the four seasons of the year, (Spring, Summer, Autumn, Winter). The mind and body is no exception. Life is a fascinating journey; the journey begins at birth, and we do know that the journey will end when the last breath leaves its dwelling place, (the body). Each moment comes with the wonderful breath that takes us into the inevitable. Life is indeed, the world's most intriguing phenomenon.

Thankfulness

Thankfulness is a humane gesture that represents appreciation of kindness. A simple **thank you** can compensates for the resentment from someone whose act of kindness went unrecognized. A deserving recognition for a pain's taking effort is worthy of acknowledgement. When thankfulness is express, it gives a feeling of satisfaction and self worth. While carefully observing the outcome of rendered deeds, the record determines its worth and appreciation that should be expressed in verbal recognition. It is often necessary to give some form of encouragement that will enhance self worth. Working toward a goal, sometimes requires focus and determination as well as assistance from others to help prepare the way for a positive outcome. With thankfulness in mind, verbal expression of thanks may be the only reward available to show appreciation for helping hands, and hearts. If a job is worth the time spent to fulfill its goal, then that job should be recognize by those who reap the benefit. Sometimes all that the recipient can offer is heart-felt thanks, which is an outward showing of humane gesture that reveals the inner thoughts.

Many kind acts get its reward by the showing of a thankful attitude from the recipient of the kindness. It is interesting to note how some noble acts of kindness goes into forgetful pages, to become unsung heroes. The determined factor that makes the difference in appreciating results of acts of kindness is simply response of recognition. I have seen people show their thankfulness in great emotional sobs when they become overwhelmed with the showing of their joyous thankfulness.

As a motor vehicle operator, I once experienced getting into the danger of misjudging my right of way, which was very scary. That incident kept me very alert; in paying attention to road codes, as I travel. If it appears as though a fellow motorist did not observe what is known to be the proper road code, when we narrowly escaped what could have been an accident, I in my conscious awareness give thanks to God, to be spared from what could have been a deadly collision.

There are many references in God's holy book (The Bible), which refers to thankfulness. One of these reference, is found in the book of

(Ephesians chapter 5:4), which reads as follows, "*Giving thanks always for all things, unto God the Father, in the name of our Lord Jesus Christ*". There will always be something for which to be thankful. We can begin by being thankful for the air that we breathe. God's Creation is beautiful in all areas of the world: we do not have to look very far, it is everywhere around us, all we have to do is to give recognition, and be thankful. The logic in this whole matter is, to show appreciation, which allows everyone concerned, to maintain a true and peaceful spirit of acceptance and acknowledgement. It is a good thing for children to be taught at an early age, how to learn about the value of thankfulness. As I grow older and come face to face with the aging process, I realize more each day how important it is to be thankful for things that I would at a younger age, take for granted, including my health. I look at youths indulging in laziness and promiscuity, and I shudder to even imagine the downfall of those who indulge in such behavior, because I see it as the future of a declining generation, that can only result in the weakening of their future progress. I thank God for those who are in favor of a moral standard, and who work hard to help make our world the kind of place that can be likened to living in a home where there is harmony, clean living, and understanding.

Thoughtlessness toward other people's feelings, and of their liberty, is something that can ruin friendship. It can also create unrest with a community of people, whose lives gets touched by the results of careless and thoughtless acts and words. To be thoughtful of others is like acknowledging the equal rights principles in action. I can appreciate the song that goes like this; ***"let there be peace on earth, and let it begin with me";*** we live and occupy our own personal space here on earth, in our existence, yet it sometimes gets quite difficult to get along with each other, because of thoughtlessness. Our world is plagued with various complexities, but while we can, "let us be kind one to another", in our own individual space."

Opinion

Every individual is entitled to voicing his or her opinion; but not all opinions are practical and safe to copy, especially when the opinion transmits a lack of reasonable comprehension. An individual's opinion may reflect an ethic of strength, based on what the opinion of the individual reveals. However, when the opinion needs to have acceptance from others who may be involved in a decision making process, there is no guarantee that the opinion expressed by one person, will meet everyone's approval. There may be a need to make changes, or to modify the idea that the opinion transmits, in order to reach a settled agreement by the group. Behavioral pattern is an outward imagery, to show the world what to expect from an individual. Usually, it is required of someone to behave in the proper manner, especially if the individual has had training to know the right behavior. Because, when the ugly flawed face of bad behavior shows up, it declares its presence of embarrassment, in the most unacceptable manner, which may happen at the wrong time, and the wrong place. There is a code of ethic, known as etiquette, of which everyone needs to be aware. If used in the proper manner, it will display good deliveries, and acceptance from others. It is not possible to understand everything there is to know about individuals in dealing with them, so we do our best to get along together in the best possible way. My observation about life, while living with other people, is that there is no one in the world who can take on the role of leadership, and will be able to solve problems totally, when dealing with a community of people. People do not always agree together about the same matter. Sometimes the simplest transaction will take a long time for people of a community to agree with their leader/s about. If there is disagreement with the simplest matter, it sometimes takes common sense to handle some of the every-day matters, in order to get the intended message across with little or no hard feelings. Let us therefore bear in mind that no one in this world is ever going to be perfect.

Life

Where there is a human beginning, there is also an inevitable end that is attached to each life; and there is no guarantee on how, where, or when the end will come. Life is time that each individual spends on planet earth. I acknowledge every moment of every day of my life as a precious gift from God. **Proper use of time can produce purposeful rewards.** The process of learning and training to do exploit, is knowledge: which is a matter of personal choice.

One of the many lessons that I learn as I advance in age, is not to reveal some of my problems that I face from time to time; because no matter how gigantic the problems appear to present themselves, somehow they always pass. Challenges great or small, will show their face every now and then in life. The unexpected, whatever that may be, does not choose a right or wrong time to make its appearance. If, and when it comes, it may demand immediate attention, and action. In using good judgment and common sense, one can only prepare for the unknown by dealing adequately with the present. Therefore, one must be thoughtful of what might be possible to do, if the unexpected happen, while life still exists. This is the best possible realistic way that

I can think of, to deal with the unexpected. It is very wonderful to note that life allows an individual to claim a place in the world while setting goals, and aiming toward reaching it. Some may require hard work and self-discipline in order to reach their desired level of expectation. As the old saying goes, "where there is a will, there is a way". The important approach is taking the first step with a prayer.

There is also another expression that gives this wise advise---"don't hang your basket higher than where your hand can reach it". There is quite a bit of logic in that statement. One example is, "don't spend more than you earn" you will land in insurmountable debt.

Each person has his or her own level of brain-power; therefore, it can be a good idea for individuals to choose the level which is better suited for them to work at, and successfully achieve. Everyone can set goals that are reachable and conducive to their ability. Remember, we are like flowers of the field of this world and we are God's great bouquet, with different colors and hues. It takes all of these flowers to fit into God's beautiful bouquet. Humans are diverse in imagery, and attribute, so "Think on these things" as we observe the handy work of God.

We humans are God's children, occupying our own special space, contained in the special body that we are born with on planet earth. Each one of us possesses our own individual spirit within our own personality that demonstrates in its special performance.

In each individual's space within the world of people, one can experience the joy of acceptance from others, as well as rejection. We should be thankful for being a one-of-a-kind individual, and try to perform at our best in our God-given ability. Our Creator expects us to fit into His wonderful bouquet on planet earth.

We learn as we journey through life, that it is important for us to have faith. Having a measure of faith is when an individual do not know for sure, but believe that there is a possibility that things hoped for can happen. However, one should not aspire to express unrealistic expectations; that can only escalate in heartbreak, when expectations, goes unfulfilled.

An individual can act with a desire to obtain, or to impart knowledge. When the intention is set into action to achieve its objectives, it can deliver positive, as well as negative results in a variety of ways. There should therefore be realistic forethought, or foresight, that disappointments can come with unexpected surprises. It is a good idea to keep that special armor of readiness, to be a shield of defense in the event of disappointments.

Training in various professional areas, produce helpful interactions that result in improved quality of every-day living, while imparting services. Good attitude of an individual can lead to rewarding advantages, which should be considered as an intent to deliver positive fulfillment to one's self, and to others people.

In every job that must be done, there can be elements of good or bad conditions. When the job seem to have unfavorable elements, but it become necessary that the job needs to be done, then it must be done regardless of its difficult challenges. There can be recognizable acknowledgements of the good, or even the bad, depending on its characterized attribution. My approach to dealing with the bad element is to carefully examine the problem regardless of the circumstance, to do what is necessary to fix it, or to eliminate the cause, in order to get past the obstruction, and move on. In the meantime, it is important to use the experiences gained from the various situation, with a desire to enjoy the deserving good that may have come from the various encounters, and make them part of the working and learning process.

The reason for working is to obtain the power of wealth, or for gaining independence, which may not necessarily mean receiving money at all times, or in all cases. It can sometimes be in the form of, working to preserve one's own environment, both in the home and outdoor surroundings. Keeping these environments clean and comfortable, makes it much more delightful to look at and enjoy.

As I worked in my flower garden one day pulling weeds and trimming the hedges, I heard a screeching sound in the overhang of shrubs. I stopped still, and carefully listened, as I intently and quietly directed my attention in finding out where the sound was coming from. As I listened and followed the sound, I discovered a tiny green grasshopper sitting on the leaf of a shrub whistling and having its own fun. As I carefully observed the tiny insect, I notice that one of the grasshopper legs were missing. As I watched, still in amazement, I thought to myself, that despite the disability of this tiny green grasshopper, it declared its ability to make its own music in its own insect-world, which attracted my attention.

Each individual's life is spent in the time and place wherever he or she happen to be, in the process of growth, and living. Life of the individual demonstrates its value by acquainting its total person with thoughts that produces ideas, and its ideals. Whatsoever these accumulation of thoughts, and ideas reveals, will be expressed in the showing of attitudes, actions, and verbal delivery, good or bad. No one is ever able to graduate from the learning process, as long as life is present in it natural form. I see myself as a candidate for learning, and that will continue until I breathe no more.

It is quite possible for me to envision unrealistic expectations by allowing myself to believe in something that I know is not humanly possible for me to do. For instance, I know that at age 75, I cannot run a race that I could run at age 15, because I do not have the stamina and physical strength at this my golden age, but I have other qualities that I did not have at an early stage of life. Factually speaking, I could not write my idea in book form at age 15, and expect to have it published, because my brain was not yet fully developed; and the opportunity for me to write was unheard of at that age and stage of my life. However, as I grow and develop into adulthood, I have grown into understanding what I can or cannot do. I do acknowledge that the knowledge I have accumulate in the process of living and learning can be compiled in a transmittable story for someone else to read, and know about.

As an orphan at a very tender age, I encountered many change of residences. At one point of my young life, moving to and from care-givers, I fell short of having a real home-life or family stability. During that period of my life, I needed someone who could have taken the responsibility of caring about the little details of my needs, and who would consider my interest of getting a good education, which did not happen. Therefore, something as important as putting words into the action of writing a book during those early years of my life never entered my mind.

I learned through living, and listening. In the early stages, opportunities were hard to come by in my environment. However, in my twenties while living in my native country, (Jamaica) I became fortunate to obtain a job as a receptionist.

The fact is, the owner of the place took a liking to me, and took it on herself to teach and train me for the job. Perhaps the only good thing I had going for me besides getting the job, was my good looks and healthy body. I had a 4th grade education at that time, but as an orphan, I carried a prayer in my heart and the good Lord took care of my heart.

I refer my experiences of training for that job, like that of the Israelites going to the Promise Land by way of the desert. I took the opportunity to listen and learn and that I did very well. At that phase of my life I could be classified as an (Eliza Do'Little), that is portrayed in the movie "My Fair Lady," although in fact, mine was a different culture.

I remember having to change shift with a coo-worker who was a Judge's daughter, and who went to one of the best schools in the country (Jamaica) and had a college education, did not see the value of that job as I did. Because to me the unexpected happened, when my employer trained me for the job, and I considered her to be, my Good Samaritan. One day after speaking with my coo-worker about something that she needed to know on starting her shift did not seem to register properly with her when I delivered the information. In her response to my information, she politely said to me, "Sadie, you are talking backwards!" will you please explain it to me again. That was a wake-up call for me, and I became aware, as well as a bit shaken by her frank statement, that I needed to sharpen up my act of learning to speak proper English in clear statement. That carried its warning signal to me. I stayed on my toes after that encounter and I worked on my English vocabulary. I might respectfully add that I worked on that job for four interesting years.

During that four years period of my life, I had the opportunity of meeting people from different parts of the world, and I learned a lot, and gained experience that would serves as stepping-stones, to enter other adventures.

Although I did lack a formal education, as soon as I was able to fend properly for myself, I realized the importance of knowledge. Even though I was not able to go to school full time, I took home study courses, while working at several odd jobs. I broaden my horizon by listening, as well as try to choose my words carefully. I have learned to, think before I speak. I worked hard, and did my best to become independent. You can read about my adventures through life in my Autobiography, (The Other Side Of Sadie) published by (AuthorHouse.com).

There are limitations in everyone's life: because no one individual can do all the daily requirements that are necessary to sustain all the needs of life's existence on earth. I accept the challenge of my life by working hard, in areas of my capability: with a determination to prove my point. My point is: my willingness to do the best that I can in whatsoever job I am engaged in doing, that I am capable of doing. In my experience of dealing with people of different language and culture, I find that it is sometimes interesting, even intimidating. Standing aside and observing the outward showing and expression of an ill-tempered individual, exploding in rage is not a welcomed experience. Rage, to me is an inner feeling that expresses itself in an outward emotion of unrest, which can result in a noisy, or violent performance. The warning signal for me as a bystander is to stay away from the enraged individual/s, and avoid becoming involved in the chaotic situation. I have seen demonstrations of angry mobs that senselessly attack innocent people who are just bystanders. Many such attacks result in injuries, and even loss of lives. Some anger appears to be very deceptive and senseless.

In these trying times with its various complexities, we must be aware of facts, that life produces various types of individuals, with various types of behavioral pattern, even though we live in the same world and even the same culture, we are a people of diverse thinking, as well as capabilities.

Individuals with specialized skills who perform at their level of contributing to society, their occupations are required for the maintenance of life on earth. It takes all types of skills and services together to preserve a life of wholeness for everyday living.

No matter how hard I try, I sometimes seem to fall short of reaching the level of total perfection in many things that I do, or visualize myself as being good at doing. Because I always see someone who I think has done better than whatever it is that I perceive as my best. Nevertheless, after doing my best to get to what I perceive as my best, it satisfies me that I give myself the benefit of trying to do my best.

Any failure that I may encounter in my effort to be my best, is my responsibility to think through, and to see whether or not there is any possibility, to do better. Bearing in mind that every individual has his or her own God given uniqueness in the many different areas of life, an opportunity to try is always an open door. Even though not everyone can have the opportunity to achieve higher education in life, as long as there is health and strength, there is something in this world to get hold of, and do as best as possible in that area, to show the worth of living, and achieving.

Understanding

Understanding is a very important aspect of an individual's awareness and ability to comprehend. As soon as a child begins the process of speaking, the requirement to understand begins with listening, which in turn directs and shapes that individual's personality. Examples are: right versus wrong information, which begins when the individual is capable of understanding the culture and language of their environment, and learning to adapt. The law and the constitutional order of the governing body of that country, is the order by which to obey the rules that are already established.

An early beginning of a child's life, in learning to say and do what is right from wrong gives the direction to understanding. Knowing the meaning of what is right at the early stage of life will give valuable control to help the individual in and out of the home environment, to deal with judging between good, and bad. This will also serve as guideline to fit into the individual's cultural environment.

I believe it is imperative at an early stage of life to get the training that will lead in a positive direction for every-day living. When the mind is young, it is vulnerable in grasping what the eyes see, and what the ears hear.

Although each Nation of the world has its particular language and dialects that fits its culture, it can also adapt to speaking many other languages outside of its environment, by means of training individuals through the educational system. Individuals must be willing to accept training, in order to allow the mind to develop in understanding of a new language, which in turn will provide the required knowledge. Language concept is usually a barrier that is difficult to grasp and understand in the beginning training, and may be easier to grasp and learn while living and interacting with people in the new culture. Every culture relates to the principles of its own governing body. (Psalm 119, in the King James version of the Holy bible), speaks these words; **"Let my cry come near before you Oh Lord: Give me Understanding according to thy Word."** God has allowed Humankind, through His Divine mercy, to advance in the knowledge of understanding science, and technology. We should therefore do our best to acknowledge and honor His Deity, and treat life with understanding, toward each other, according to His Word.

I have experienced crushing disappointment, that left me feeling beaten and bewildered, which sometimes take me some time to shake off. Nevertheless, I see myself with enough life in me to start something new. When I sometimes feel physically weakened, I understand that I may need to rest, and change my method of approach to tackle my new venture. Rest gives renewed strength in both the physical and the mental. When I am able to look back at my fears of disappointments that I conquered, I am able to allow myself willingness to appreciate the things I worked hard to accomplish, including my understanding to develop strength of character.

One of my willingness to overcoming a disappointment caused by an individual is to carefully think through the matter that created the problem. I try to deal with the conflict in my heart in order to make the ultimate decision of forgiving the individual who have done me wrong. In the process of my making the decision, I relieve myself of anxieties, by clearing my mind of blame. The most rewarding influence that I find to be comforting is prayer and praise to God; because it offers peaceful consolation that can be done while taking time to rest. While journeying through life, I realize how much there is that I can learn, even through rest time and meditation. I have learned that it is the thought process that evaluates, and relays, right and wrong influences; and influences, creates the good or bad action. Even a late bloomer can learn with dignity, and be pleased with the good thoughts, revealed in spoken words. Therefore, as a late bloomer, my encouragement to folks, both the young and the aged, is to exercise their God given ability by making good use of time to deliver a message that will enhance someone who is hurting mentally or physically. Speaking words of worth can relay messages to many people of the world, to heal wounded hearts, and create environments of peace.

Delays

Delays can happen in every conceivable area of life's transactions; and every person will experience some form of it at some time and point of a lifetime. The real test is to deal appropriately with the setbacks of delays, and try to maintain control while moving on. No one was born knowing every thing; the first thing a baby learns to do is what comes naturally, and that is to cry on entering into earth's environment. Every person that enters the world learns during the growth process of living. Those who have lived and occupied earth before us, taught those who followed, and so the cycle of teaching and learning continues throughout the journey that we know as life. Individuals learn from each other: and some develop their own method of expertise and skill to share with the world.

Everyone sometimes encounter changes, that may affect his/her mood, and mood change can happen in the every-day transactions of life; which may be caused by sickness, loneliness, resentful behavior from others, and a host of other eventualities. One can sit and bring to mind past pains that had hurt in dramatic ways, but it is dangerous to mope over failures of the past when the new day can offer hope and renewal. It is said that, "history turns on small hinges". Development of character comes from years of living. Experiences can accumulate during living and learning in a timely manner. Life is an incredible asset given to human beings by God, the Creator. Many individuals take full advantage of living, while making great contribution to the world in which we live. During the process of these individuals making their valuable recognizable contributions for themselves in serving the public, they may in the process, develop the title of being a celebrity.

One may say, well, "their hinges must have gotten special greasing;" and that may be true; nonetheless, whichever way it happens it may be seen as note-worthily and acceptable. It takes hard work and lots of discipline, to acquire the achieved knowledge that fulfills the level of accomplishment. Discipline is required to do what is right even when the going gets rough. It may not be over, even when the desired level to a goal is reach: it is the contribution made by the individual during the duration of continued work done, that has to be considered as valuable. Say for example: an individual pursue training in higher education to become a physician: in order to reach the goal of becoming a qualified medical doctor is not where the story ends. The progression of hard work and continuous study carries its own distinction, while the individual moves forward, to become worthy of recognition.

I really applaud those who sets goals and work toward fulfilling the mission; bearing in mind that countless hours are spent studying to gather information that must be stored in the mind, in order to reach the level of the acquired knowledge that is necessary to fulfill the plan. Every mission begins with an idea. When that first thought gives birth, the suggested idea begins to take shape, which many times turns out to begin its expansion process that escalates into a far greater dimension than was originally imagined.

When the tragedy of the Space Shuttle "Challenger" happened on January 28, 1986, killing all seven Crew Members, President Ronald Reagan on delivering his message to the nation, made this statement; "The future doesn't belong to the fainthearted; it belongs to the brave: the Challenger's Crew were pulling us into the future, and we will continue to follow them". I truly believe that-- "Brave hearts will never be satisfied until the battle is won, and victory is declared".

Aiming to win

When individuals venture out into educational studies to pursue academic advancement whether in commerce, to achieve professional diplomas and degrees, or even to obtain athletic recognition: their aim is to win. There are many areas and levels within the educational arena from which to choose. Education is truly an open thoroughfare for those who dare to take the challenge.

The real test is, choosing the area of study that is best suited for the individual's mental, and physical ability. In this world of people with many ideas, values, hopes and dreams, individuals can find their rightful place in society, when they venture out with hope and expectation to achieve favorable outcome. While an individual journey through the educational thoroughfare to seek success in the area chosen for study, there is always going to be a procedure that will declare the ultimate result of success or failure. Education involves people, in every conceivable areas of occupational transaction: which means that there is always going to be an individual's expectation of **aiming to win**. Winning is the result of hard work and countless hours of study-time while pursuing a goal with the determination to get to the level of acceptance. In this process, the world watches, and waits, to see the outcome. Then they will give their approval or disapproval of whatever they see, or what they perceive. Aiming to win can turn out to be a controversial debate because there are different levels of winning. The discriminating pursuer, learn to give of their best, and accept the outcome in whatever area of pursuit they take upon themselves. By stretching their extra reserve of endurance, and giving that endeavor their best possible effort, to them, winning is accepting the challenge, and giving it their best possible effort. They may not reach the best performance level of acceptance but at least they tried. I see winning as a concept, of accepting a challenge, and giving that pursuit the best effort possible.

The race in life is never over to them that refuse to quit trying. It takes faith and courage to listen to the voice of the unseen, in the process of aiming to win. As one ventures out not knowing what the final outcome of the adventure will deliver, there will be a desire, as sure as there is light, and darkness, a daring drive to pursue in the rank, of **Aiming to Win.**

One of America's famous President (Theodore Roosevelt) in 1907, made this statement: *"Far better it is to dare mighty things, than to take rank with those poor spirits who never enjoy much, because they live in the grey twilight that knows not victory nor defeat."* I do declare that, it takes faith and courage to listen to the voice of the unseen, in the pursuit of **Aiming to Win.**

Retirement

Retirement declares the final stage of job responsibility for those who spent years working and learning to acquire training while tackling an individual occupation of choice. Those who entered into the working world, who choose to pursue their life's dream and reach that noble stage of retirement, can look forward to enjoy quiet times and lazy moments. For those individuals who are fortunate to look back and remember the many challenges, good or bad, and who has come through successfully, they can truly say, "**Victory is Sweet**". However, Life at that stage do not always offer all individuals the same joys of retirement; yet, in whatever circumstance it happen, there is definitely a time to think and reflect on retirement as the final faze of their individual work-life.

Another aspect of retirement is to change from one occupation to something new. Time, and time again I find myself observing changes in my endeavors, which beacons me to be courageous in my journey through life. I see life as a continuous diversion of activities, that presents itself from day to day, and each day offers a job to do, even with spoken words. The months of May and June 2006 had been significant and meaningful for me, as I had the honor of attending graduation celebration parties of (4) four students. Two of the students were my own granddaughters, one graduated from College and the other from high school. The College graduate studied to be in the nursing profession, and had already signed a contract to work in a City hospital; the other was on her way to enter college. I was also delighted to be at (2) two of those graduates celebration party; who I nurtured and cared for in my day-care nursery when they were infants.

They all seemed very excited, and full of enthusiasm toward their future, and I was thrilled to have the opportunity to be with them for such important events. All of those young people were on their way to job or college, with great hope for themselves in their quest for further advancement, with willingness to explore possibilities. Things changes with time, and change is a constant thing that happens in everyone's daily lives. Change is the one thing that we all have in common.

No one can graduate out of life, because life and time is constantly changing things: allowing opportunities, by which to explore and produce, with new changes. My encouragements to those who are ready to explore possibilities, is that they should release their god-given talents and spend quality time to study and expand in their horizon. To believe in themselves for their development as they set goals. If there had been mistakes of the past, learn from them: and develop wisdom to improve self-image. Every new day brings with it new ideas to evaluate and set in their proper perspective. I truly believe that it takes hard work and a determination to overcome obstacles. With the desire to pursue a set goal, and willingness to give it the best effort possible, something good that relates to achievement, will happen. It is important to embrace dignity, creativity, and clean living; but most of all recognition to the worship of God who is Creator of all things:

giving Him honor and praise in all areas of endeavors: expectation to have good thing happen in the process of making the effort to try, will bear healthy fruits.

Memory

Memory is influence of a powerful thought process that can reflect the behavioral pattern of an individual. It is the sole responsibility of the individual to control his or her deliveries that the memory present. Sometimes my memory gets stubborn to be controlled; because of the compelling force that evolves, and seem to take up residency in the subconscious that make its appearance without a formal invitation. It can be difficult to shake off some memories easily, but I refuse to become hostage of un-welcomed memories that threatens my mental frame of mind to make destructive deliveries. When one of those disruptive memories pops up to threaten and interrupt my pleasant moment, I quickly disperse and replace it with a pleasant thought that is close on hand. A good thought is always ready and available to replace the unwanted memory. This method really works for me and I highly recommend it to anyone who may experience the danger of that un-welcomed phenomenon that I make mention of.

I consider my mind to be a great storehouse for my memory. It stores happy memories as well as sad memories while I pass through time each day. Although my mind seems only to register the most dramatic events, as well as things that I purposely want to remember, some memory leaves its indelible mark on my life that has remained in the subconscious and will pop up when I least expect. There are those unwanted memories that I must give my attention. They all seem to be there, hidden in a corner of my existence, to remind me that I am still capable of asserting this precious part of me. My mind communicates ideas with my thought process, allowing me to prove its existence in the things I do and say, it also allows me to communicate, when I interact with people.

Memory can be marred with a disease known as forgetfulness, which sometimes happens to people at an old age. It is quite distressing for someone who unfortunately suffers from brain complications that leads to mental illness. Otherwise, a normal functional individual can have memories that are stored in a corner of their mind that has the potential to experience pop ups, at unexpected moments.

Some individuals are blessed to possess a photographic memory that enables them to store and accumulate a great deal of information that they can click on with incredible speed at all times. Human voice is also scientifically place in equipments such as robots that are in many of today's services worldwide. Many household appliances have built-in control system that can operate on coded memory. We live in a fast pace world of memory, whether or not it is human related, or mechanically relayed: memory has become an absolute necessity. We should therefore give thanks for this incredible resource known as memory.

Circumstances

Circumstances are conditions that may affect an individual's life. One of which is a circumstance surrounding a life at birth, which a child faces on entering into the world. Conditions at that early stage can be good, as well as unfortunate, and can affect the growth process. No child has asked to be born; this miracle is an act of God that He designed, into being at the time when He spoke the universe into existence, and created man and woman to occupy and take care of everything on earth. According to the Holy Scripture in the (King James version) as states, in *Genesis 1- 27: 28,* reads as follows—"*So God Created Man in his own image. In the image of God created he him; male and female created he them. And God blessed them, and God said unto them, be fruitful, and multiply, and replenish the earth, and subdue it: and have dominion over the fish of the sea, and over the fowl of the air, and over every living thing that moveth upon the earth*".

Thus with the connection of man and woman, the close encounter of productivity is in compliance with God's plan for man and woman to create offspring. God has predestined conception to be this way since His Creation of human beings, and the natural process continues throughout human existence. Every human being falls into the same category of, "being born". The financial circumstance of an individual birth can vary in terms of being born to a wealthy family, or being born to a poor family. Looking at its general prospective in today world, one would have to say that the child who is born within the wealthy family has automatically become heir to the wealth of their rich family's possessions depending on the principles and policies of that group. That child can therefore capitalize on the fame and fortune of their heritage, thus making their journey through life financially less stressful to handle, if carefully managed. The child who is born to a poor family sometimes enters into the world bearing the scars of lacking many provisions that could allow much needed amenities that are essential to proper growth and development.

Financially speaking, the poor child will have a much more difficult journey through life, than the one born to the wealthy family. Nevertheless, some of the ills of being born poor can be less stressful with the devotion of tender loving care from family and friends, pooling resource together to create the village in raising the child, which in turn enforces strength in character, and for a nurturing support system.

The poor child can grow to overcome the turbulence of poverty, and achieve wealth through hard work and a determination to excel, and win the war against poverty. These are some true-to-life circumstances relating to many individual lives in our world. There is an old saying that says, "*where there is a will there is a way*;" the truth of that matter is, that a person must first possess the will, that can lead the way to make success happen in the area of which the desired goal is being pursued.

Personally speaking, I have committed my will, to keep a covenant with my Heavenly Father (GOD). The covenant of that will is, to give Him   praise, and to worship Him, for as long as I can breathe and think, and have my being. Many of my past encounters have, in many ways influence my present concepts of choice. I have learned through living, that I should not get complacent in my pursuit to experience inner peace. I understand that those experiences gained have allowed me to accumulate wisdom; which has enabled me to choose what I believe is best for my present encounters. I am thereby satisfied to know that I can trust the will that I possess, to help direct me in the way that I believe is best for my present circumstance.

Each moment gives me renewed hope to keep on striving toward what may be the best that hope-fully will happen. It is therefore my daily duty to prepare myself both mentally and physically for that which I have not yet seen; so that I can be ready to even take a licking, and keep on ticking, while clinging to "my will to find the way. The many incredible uses of science and technology, offers training and increased knowledge to those who are able to take advantage of the various opportunities that are available. Yet misuse of many of these knowledge that were meant to be for the good of life, are being used destructively to harm the existence humankind. For example, Air Planes were design to get from point A to point B. not to be use to deliberately plunge into buildings to kill innocent people. There are now missiles and rockets that can wipe out a community of people within minutes. Satellites and wireless communications connect with radio, and television that transmits news, and to relay visual pictured details around the world within seconds. "Goodness gracious!" "look how far human's ingenuity has come!"   Knowledge has excelled with the passing of time: and there is no telling how much further it will progress.

Impact

My opinion of the word **Impact** is, that it is a word often use to describe the intensity of action with regards to words, and acts that can affect individuals in remarkable and unforgettable ways. One day while having a conversation with a close member of my family I was confronted with a comments made to me that, "*you don't know the **Impact** that you have made on numerous people*". That comment got me thinking, and as my thoughts reflected, I could not help but remembering some good, and some not so good memories: and I wondered how much good or bad **impact** I have contributed to one or many lives. On August 6, 1965, President L. Johnson signed into law, the Voting Rights Act that gives black people of the U.S.A. the right to cast their vote, in Order to make their voices heard. That had a tremendous **impact** of good will on the lives of all black Americans from that time on, and answer to prayers of the Civil Rights movement under the leadership of (Dr. Martin Luther King Jr.)

The **Impact** that creates influences can transfer or impart messages that send its rippling effect along its path, as conceived by way of eyes, ears and mouth. It can create numerous messages that are capable of delivering joy or sadness in the process of its perception. I would like to think that my words and action delivers meaningful influences. I also know that I have inherited valuable lessons that have been passed on by really interesting individuals. Therefore, I do my best to honor the memory of those folks who delivers noble deeds, and words, from which I can acquire inspiration and knowledge.

Another use of this word **Impact** is that it can also describe the effects of tragedies such as accidents that may be the cause of collision, natural disasters, or sudden dramatic encounters good or bad. Such a small word, that offers such a variety of usage. In his memorable Inaugural Address to the nation of, United States of America President John Fitzgerald Kennedy (J.F.K) said: *"And so my fellow Americans, ask not what your country can do for you, ask what you can do for your country; ask not what America can do for you, but what together we can do for the freedom of man."* Those words are food for thoughts.

One of the memories that linger with me, seemed also to have had a dramatic impact on an entire Nation of people; it was the assassination of President Kennedy on November 22, 1963, 12:30 P.M. while traveling in a motorcade through a street in Dallas, Texas, U. S. A. The news quickly spread around the world through the media of radio and television. People all over the country and around the world, were left in amazement, and shock. This was an unprecedented era in the making of recorded history: that was destined to create a lifestyle of change for many people.

Today September 11, 2006, marks five (5) years since the terrorist attack on America when some terrorist overpowered Pilots on four passenger Jet Air Planes: plunging the first, and second plane into the Twin towers of the New York Trade Center, the third plane in the Washington D.C Pentagon, and the fourth plane into a Pennsylvania field.   That sudden and dramatic impact of the disaster left the entire nation in shock and disbelief.   Today, Americans are encouraged to observe a few moments of silence in honor of those who died.   Those who managed to escape will never forget the horror of their experience. Today, five years later, family members and friends are still grieving. The after effect of this great tragedy has change the way people travel, and it has done great harm to the country's freedom and economy, while upsetting lives of a great number individuals.   These are changing times, and I can say that I live to see so many changes take place around the world..   So many dramatic occurrences that happen in my lifetime, makes me think of the proverb that says, "***Tomorrow is promised to no one;**" no one knows what any tomorrow will bring; we should therefore work together to help create an environment, suitable for the good of humanity while life on this planet exists.

Short Memos

When the wings of love is broken
It flip-flops round and round
Until it loses all of its power
Then the love willingly dies

It is interesting how a mind
will create its own fantasies.
Only the individual's mind
Understands the extent
Of its Imaginary Journey.

"Politeness is to do and say
The kindest things
In the kindest ways."

Excellence in all its splendor
can be seen in sincere deeds
With its noblest contribution
Polished with a thought of love

Where we go from here
Is by taking the first step
To where we need to go

To love and trust Jesus Christ
Is to obey God the Father
In acknowledgement
Of His Holy Words

Treat God's World with respect
Enjoy its beauty all around
By helping to keep it clean

There is nothing on earth
That is as valuable as Gods Word
Give it due respect, and seek after it.

Resolve the grief that hurts you
Tell your troubles to Dr. Jesus
And seek the cure in his word
I heard a songbird singing
In the middle of the night
I could not believe my ear
It was a pleasant phenomenon!!

The miracle of childbirth
Is to hear a baby's first cry
On entering the unknown

When emotion is spills over in tears
Loosen up and let it flow
Then cry to your heart's content

If the heart have a song
Then make your own music
Sing with joy and gladness
And let your voice be heard

Lord fill my heart with wisdom
And conform the thoughts in me
So to be worthy of your trust
I hereby strive to do your will

To see, to hear, to speak,
To smell and taste; these five
Senses, makes the heart glad!

The battlefield of human-beings lies
within the heart, to fight the force
of evil, that shows its ugly face

Children are eager to learn
Help them build their confidence
By setting good examples in place

Pass along each bounteous Blessing
That may come to you through life
You may help a weary traveler
Who grows faint amid the strife.

Sincerely,
Sadie N. Williams.

About the Author

"Ms. Williams is a prolific writer who has not allowed the hardships of manuscripts lost through floods, and other set-backs to deter her spirit. Her life story and her poetic imagery has been shared with and enjoyed by fellow church members, family and friends.

Her new effort, she tries her hand at a stream-of-consciousness approach, allowing her thoughts to flow freely on a number of common subjects of interest to her. Her faith in God, love of nature and belief in people shines through in this work as in her earlier writings."

(Mary S. Newby)

Notes

Notes

Notes

Notes

Notes

To Purchase these books
Email—promisechildrens@wmconnect.com
Or- authorhouse.com
Autobiography: The Other Side of Sadie
This Side of Sadie's Co-Terminal
Sadie's Thoughts in Poetry and Prose

www.ingramcontent.com/pod-product-compliance
Lightning Source LLC
Chambersburg PA
CBHW031240280526
45784CB00004B/1661